Jesus' Epilogue To The Sermon On The Mount

A Study Of
The Lord's Prayer

Charles E. Link

CSS Publishing Company, Inc.
Lima, Ohio

JESUS' EPILOGUE TO THE SERMON ON THE MOUNT

Library of Congress Cataloging-in-Publication Data

Link, Charles E., 1927-
    Jesus' epilogue to the Sermon on the mount : a study of the Lord's prayer / Charles E. Link.
        p.   cm.
    ISBN 0-7880-0374-7
    1. Lord's prayer — Study and teaching. 2. Sermon on the mount — Study and teaching. I. Title.
BV230.L47   1995
226.9'6'007—dc20   94-24369
                                                                          CIP

This book is available in the following formats, listed by ISBN:
0-7880-0374-7 Book
0-7880-0375-5 IBM 3 1/2 computer disk
0-7880-0376-3 IBM 3 1/2 book and disk package
0-7880-0377-1 Macintosh computer disk
0-7880-0378-X Macintosh book and disk package
0-7880-0379-8 IBM 5 1/4 computer disk
0-7880-0380-1 IBM 5 1/4 book and disk package

PRINTED IN U.S.A.

In memory of

Clarence A. Nipper

whose theological hunger
included intellectual honesty
and human compassion.

Contents

Part 2
Our Role In The Realm Of God

How To Use This Book

Though *Jesus' Epilogue To The Sermon On The Mount* serves well as a book for individual inspiration and instruction, it is designed in such a way that it may be used as a supplement to Thomas Short's book of sermons on the Lord's Prayer, *A New Hearing Of An Old Prayer,* and as a guide for a class of adults wishing to focus on the major themes of the Sermon on the Mount/Plain, as found in Matthew 5-7 and Luke 6.

"Research Activities" and "For Discussion" segments have been interspersed at significant places in the text for the convenience of study leaders. More "Questions For Discussion" will be found at the end of each chapter.

An individual or group using this guide book simultaneously with a pastor's sermon series on the Lord's Prayer will find their appreciation for these important segments of Jesus' teaching considerably enlarged and deepened.

It is possible to be selective with these lessons. For example, the book is divided into two parts of six lessons each (a "study unit" as frequently practiced today in adult education formats). In addition, chapters four through six, about God's sovereignty, power and glory, lend themselves to a short "retreat" format. The frequent references to the Lord's Prayer make this book a useful supplement to a Lord's Prayer sermon series, as is suggested by the publisher in making this book a companion piece to *A New Hearing Of An Old Prayer.*

The reader will notice that the author shares the concern of many today to find gender neutral terms for God and the Kingdom of God. The uniqueness and complexity of God's divine nature and sovereignty will continue to elude our limited and gender specific vocabulary. In this book, "him" and "his" in reference to God is avoided by a simple repetition of "God," and "God's Realm" is substituted for "God's Kingdom."

However this book is utilized, it is the author's hope that readers will be challenged to take the Master Teacher's instructions about God and our manner of life within the Realm of God more seriously.

Introduction

. Through the centuries, in its diligent effort to proclaim and defend biblical claims for the divine nature of Jesus, Christianity has inadvertently minimized His significance as the Spokesman for God's Realm and Teacher of that Realm's principles, ethics and affirmations. The practical result of this is that modern Christians, with but rare exceptions, have not taken seriously the ethical implications of the Sermon on the Mount's powerful and culture-challenging teachings. These lessons on Jesus' teachings about God's Realm may help correct this distortion by looking at the teachings of Jesus from the perspective of the transformation in human life and relationships that He came to achieve.

We do this by approaching the Sermon on the Mount through the "lens" of the Lord's Prayer, suggesting that as the Beatitudes are the prologue to the Sermon, the Lord's Prayer is its epilogue.

This approach gives us a whole new perspective! No longer is the Lord's Prayer simply a useful piece of ritual. It may provide an occasion for *signing on* to the morally demanding and culture-countering ethics of the Sermon of which it is a central part.

Greater attention needs to be given to the context in which the Lord's Prayer is found. Questions we need to ask are: What was Jesus' purpose in giving us these teachings? What do they imply for perception of God and for our ethical behavior?

We must study again the teachings of Jesus and hear, as if for the first time, the call for us to be peacemakers, to have a mellowing effect on the world, to stand for honesty, truthfulness, integrity and loyalty in human relationships; to practice our faith and worship God not in order to impress others but "in spirit and in truth," and to give the unexpected response to enemies, exploiters and those in authority.

It is time to return to Jesus' call for His followers to be salt, light and leaven, not separating themselves from the world, but living out Jesus' radiant ethics and values in the environment where they live! The beginning of doing that is to take seriously again His challenging teachings, especially as they are announced in the Sermon on the Mount and encapsulated in Jesus' "epilogue" to the Sermon on the Mount, the Lord's Prayer.

Erik Routley has described three goals that have guided him through the years as a preacher, musician and historian: 1) to arouse in an unbiblical generation a love for the Bible and a wish to make friends with it; 2) to assure people that the scriptures have something to say about what they themselves find perplexing or delightful; and 3) to awaken a conviction that, in Christ, life is worth living.

The same objectives have guided this author and he has striven to hold up the practical as well as the spiritual implications of the Sermon on the Mount and its "epilogue," the Lord's Prayer.

Charles E. Link
1994

Part 1
The Realm Of God

Chapter 1

Jesus As Teacher Of The Realm Of God

Luke 6:46-49

In its understandable effort to defend the divine nature of Jesus, the Church has tended through the centuries to minimize the equally important significance of Jesus as the Teacher of God's truth, Spokesman for the Kingdom of God.

Such inadvertent downplaying of Jesus as teacher appears in the early creeds of the church. In the Nicene Creed and the Apostles' Creed the emphasis is upon the divine nature of Jesus; and there is no mention of his role as Teacher of the Realm of God.

While attending hearings prior to the approval of one denomination's Brief Statement of Faith, some observers were struck by the fact that there was in the draft statement no reference to Jesus' teaching ministry. Under pressure from lay people and parish pastors, the committee of theologians and institutional representatives inserted the phrase "teaching by word and deed" to a subsection dealing with Jesus as "proclaimer of the Reign of God."

The Church has been so concerned that its doctrines about Jesus be guarded that it has seemed to look with suspicion upon any attempt to emphasize the importance of Jesus as unparalleled Teacher.

The practical result of this is that modern Christians have not taken as seriously as they should the implications of Jesus' ethical admonitions and culture-challenging teachings.

Reinforcing the earliest understandings of Jesus as an unparalleled Teacher of the principles and foundational affirmations of the Kingdom of God, one biblical scholar concludes that the first followers of Jesus focused not on Jesus' divine life and destiny as "the third Person of the Trinity" but upon the social transformation called for by his teachings. They heard Jesus challenging them to live authentically in the midst of a topsy-turvy world!

Some are not adverse to thinking of Jesus, in light of these earliest impressions among the "Jesus People," as a Jewish Socrates. But in doing that, they ignore a critical aspect of Jesus' teaching: his ability to initiate change within the hearts of his listeners! This was surely a unique and divine aspect of Jesus' nature as God had given it to him, a characteristic of God that was also present in Jesus. His teachings not only reasoned people into change, but got inside those who would listen intently and began the process of change. It was surely those who found not only their minds being changed but their hearts, as well, who said of Jesus: "He teaches as one with authority and not as the scribes" (Matthew 7:29).

Research Activity

What was the disciples' reply when Jesus, early in his Galilean ministry, asked them if they would like to leave him? (See John 6:68.) What does their answer reveal about their estimate of Jesus' teaching? In the previous verse (6:63) what does Jesus say about the relationship of his words and the Spirit? How do these verses support the observation that Jesus' teachings affected more than the intellect?

The Acts of the Apostles records that those first followers were more than mere scribes of the teachings of Jesus, they experimented with life in common, selling their property and possessions, turning their backs on skeptical family and friends, risking jobs and "position in society," and, as persecution threatened, more! They understood Jesus to be calling them to a great social experiment that would better prepare them for the coming-in Realm of God. They saw themselves not as starters of a new religion but as pioneers of a new way of living, believing and relating. They were, apparently, not entirely ineffective, for it was observed by their critics that they had "turned the world upside down" (Acts 17:6)!

But when society "joined" them with Constantine's Imperial recognition, and they found themselves no longer in conflict with the government and society's elite and powerful; as counsels were convened, and "heretics" corrected by creedal and doctrinal formulations, the focus moved from modeling a new society based on the awesome principles of God's Realm as Jesus taught them, to protection of the Church and its confessions.

It is time to return to Jesus' call for his followers to be light, salt and leaven (Matthew 5:13-16, 13:33); that is, not separating themselves from the world, but living out Jesus' unique ethics and values in the environment where they live! The beginning of doing that is to take seriously again his challenging teachings, especially as they are announced in the Sermon on the Mount.

Those passages hold up humility, peaceableness, service, honesty, and the honoring of commitment in relationships. We are called to take the initiative in mending relationships and bringing reconciliation. We are asked to honor and protect a world where God "clothes the grass of the field" and "marks the sparrow's fall." We are told that, as children of a heavenly Parent, we cannot write anyone off, saying "You fool!" but must value every person as a child of God, no matter how distasteful or perverse their behavior, for God "makes his sun to shine and his rain to fall on the just and the unjust" (Matthew 5:45).

Jesus feared that there would be some who would honor him and fail to live according to his teachings, particularly those teachings that deal with our human relationships. "If you love me, keep my commandments," he urged (John 15:10). The heroes of his parables are those who stop by the road to help the fallen (Luke 10:33), and who give water to the thirsty (Matthew 25:35), even as the villains are those who pass by on the other side, give no food to the hungry, and refuse to pass on the forgiveness they have received (Matthew 18:32-33).

15

Jesus found religious exhibitionism which was void of service or compassion repugnant. The outwardly pious, self-righteous and judgmental ones felt the lash of his tongue more than any others. Whereas, those caught in sins like adultery or shady dealings received gentle admonitions in the context of significant dialogue, permeated with grace, as with Zacchaeus (Luke 19:5), the woman at the well (John 4:6), and the woman "taken in the act of adultery" (John 8:3-4).

Some accept the fact that those who originally heard Jesus with eagerness had the ability to change communicated to them along with the words. But they wonder if those who read those teachings today are affected by the same transformation.

For Discussion

Is it still true that the Teacher is yet able to change hearts as well as minds? Was there some mysterious power available to those who heard the words from the very lips of the Teacher that is not present now with the written or retold word? Who did Jesus pray for in John 17:20? How is that prayer reinforced by his promise that God would send the Spirit, the *paraclete* (John 15:26)? If you had been there, how might you have been affected by such a promise?

Still, there are those who, rather than bringing a listening heart to their study of scripture, bring an opinion or rigid position seeking biblical corroboration. Thinking they have found it, they accuse those who disagree with them of not accepting the Bible as "the word of God." They need to understand, as someone has aptly said, that the Bible is the word of God not when *I* control it but when *it* controls *me*! The secret is having a heart and mind that is willing to be taught.

To say that the Bible is the word of God when it controls me, not when I control it, is to conclude something very important about the ability of the Spirit to enable those written words to "control," transform, motivate and empower us.

16

It is still possible for the jaded world to perceive how we love and recognize that we have been with Jesus by the manner of our lives, relationships and value commitments. Perhaps we may again be observed as those who come to turn the world upside-down, with a view to setting it right-side-up!

Nels Ferré once shared with a group of pastors his belief that the reason the church has been so busy stressing the divine nature of Jesus and downplaying his humanity is that *"if Jesus is not much like us, then we don't have to be much like him."* That is a terrible indictment. It means that the call to be salt, light and leaven in the world in which we live has been virtually ignored.

It is past time to emphasize in the life of the church and in our daily lives as Christians the necessity of "walking the walk" as well as "talking the talk" (using a participant's challenge to a visiting group of church people to a drug counseling group). The world needs models more than it needs judges. It needs those who will be Jesus' disciples (students), study his word and show his love. This is as important a challenge as believing that Jesus is God with us; and, if his words are any indication, it is the best praise we can give him.

Read In Unison

Why do you call me "Lord, Lord," and do not do what I tell you? I will show you what someone is like who comes to me, hears my words, and acts on them. That one is like a man building a house, who dug deeply and laid the foundation on rock; when a flood came, the river burst against that house but could not shake it, because it had been well built. But the one who hears and does not act is like a man who built a house on the ground without a foundation. When the river burst against it, immediately it fell, and great was the ruin of that house (Luke 6:46-49 NRSV).

Questions For Further Discussion

1. What has been the practical result of the Church's inclination to downplay the identity of Jesus as Teacher of the ethics of God's Realm?

2. Where did the earliest "Jesus People" focus? How did their understanding of Jesus' teaching express itself in their individual and corporate lives?

3. How did imperial approval and recognition affect the way the Church understood and interpreted the person and teachings of Jesus?

4. Do you agree that it is time for the Church to return to Jesus' call for his followers to be light, salt and leaven? How might our priorities be affected? What might we do differently?

Chapter 2

Jesus' Sermon About God's Realm

Matthew 6:9-13, Luke 11:2-4

The two most treasured prose pieces from Jesus' teaching, the Beatitudes and the Lord's Prayer, are found within the context of the Sermon on the Mount, Matthew's great compendium of Jesus' principal teachings about the Realm of God. They are best understood within that context. Luke implies, in his arrangement, that the Beatitudes and the Prayer were, like the other teachings of Jesus, spoken at various times and on various occasions. Matthew sees the value of placing them in the context of the Sermon on the Mount, not simply for some literary effect but because they movingly summarize the major faith affirmations and ethical principles that the great Sermon lifts up. It was, I believe, an inspired way of presenting our Lord's major teachings, with the Beatitudes as the "prologue" and the Lord's Prayer as the "epilogue," so to speak.

The Beatitudes and the Lord's Prayer are more than beautiful scripture passages suitable for Sunday school memorization, as they were so often given to us in our childhood. They are to be seen in the context of faith affirmation, ethical commitment and renewal of hope.

Understanding the practical implications of the Sermon on the Mount comes to those who love God and have committed themselves to the way of living and relating described in Jesus' unparalleled teachings. It would help us to understand the importance of this Sermon as a guide to a Christian way of living if we would always see it as the preamble to a Realm which presses for fulfillment.

The fact is that these teachings have the potential for stimulating faith and prodding one on in the spiritual journey. This has always been true of the words of Jesus. They do not reason us into change but they get inside those who will listen with all of their being and begin the process of change! Jesus' words, when they fall upon good soil (i.e. receptive, truly searching), do more than change our minds, they begin to form us into children of God. It is a word that does not return unto God void, but, like the word of God at creation, causes things to happen ("Let there be light . . . and there was light" — Genesis 1:3).

This probably explains the amazement of the masses at Jesus' teaching, "For he taught as one with authority, and not as the scribes" (Matthew 7:29). He was doing more than sharing pious-sounding ideas; he was continuing God's creative process, dispensing power and motivation for rebirth, renewal, transformation and change.

None of these things can happen if we allow parts of the Sermon to be an exercise by rote, mechanically repeated in public or private ritual, going through motions that are dictated by nostalgia or custom. When we do that, we lose the Sermon as a means of instruction and a description of what behavior is like in God's Realm.

A story is told of how heavyweight champion Max Baer was requested at a prayer breakfast to lead the group in the Lord's Prayer. After a moment of embarrassing silence, Baer commenced, "Now I lay me down to sleep. I pray the Lord my soul to keep . . ."

But there is something worse than mistaking that traditional child's bedtime prayer for the Lord's Prayer. And that is to use the Sermon on the Mount as a collection of memory verses for children.

During a presidential primary campaign, one of the hopefuls was asked if he prayed, to which he replied, "Yes, we go to church four or five times a year, and we always pray there, don't we?"

Perhaps it was this very fear that caused Jesus to label his Prayer a *model* rather than a substitute for original prayers. For Matthew reports Jesus saying, "Pray in *this way*," rather than simply "Pray this prayer" (Matthew 6:9a). The distinction is important! The Bible is clear on how God feels about prayer by rote, a mechanical religious exercise.

It might well be argued from the record that Jesus was not interested in providing ritualistic prayers, at all, and that the liturgical form of the Lord's Prayer that Matthew presents is a revision of the Early Church. Look, for example, at the much simpler version of the prayer that Luke offers:

Father, hallowed be your name.
Your kingdom come.
Give us each day our daily bread.
And forgive us our sins,

for we ourselves forgive
everyone indebted to us.
And do not bring us to the time of trial.
(Luke 11:2-4 NRSV)

Immediately we notice how much shorter the Luke version is. Luke's version has nothing to correspond with Matthew's opening "our" or "in heaven" in the first line, and it omits "Thy will be done on earth as it is in heaven" and "But deliver us from evil," and it omits the doxological "For thine is the kingdom" conclusion altogether.

Research Activity

Look up *Lord's Prayer* in a Bible Dictionary and observe what is said about the two versions in Matthew and Luke. Which is probably nearer the original as Jesus gave it? Picture yourself as a persecuted Early Church member. What would the closing phrases about God's kingdom, power and glory have meant to you?

The point is that it was most likely the early Christian community that perceived the Prayer as one for liturgical use, not Jesus. We do well to respect the lead-in phrase as reported in Matthew, "Pray then *in this way.*" It is a model for Christian prayer that Jesus was offering, not a locked-in liturgical prayer.

On the other hand, we could not fault the early Christian community for including the Lord's Prayer in their liturgical development, considering the trials they had endured or were enduring as a persecuted minority within the Roman and Jewish worlds where they lived. To reaffirm faith in God's emerging kingdom and supreme will from hearts aflame with rejoicing at Christ's resurrection assured that, for them, the prayer would not be said mechanically or out of a sense of habit. It truly expressed what was in their hearts!

Except in places of similar persecution, who can confidently say that this "centerpiece" of the Sermon on the Mount is repeated with the same passion and longing in western churches today?

Attempts to respect the Sermon on the Mount context have been made. For example, some new worship books include a litany on the Lord's Prayer which may be used occasionally as a variation on the simple recitation of the Lord's Prayer. They encourage the worshipper to weigh each phrase of the prayer, exploring the meaning and significance of each petition. These are creative and thoughtful attempts to encourage us to respect the Sermon on the Mount framework for the Lord's Prayer.

We must emphasize that the Lord's Prayer is best understood within the context of the Sermon on the Mount, for it summarizes those important affirmations about God's sovereignty and parenthood and offers divine guidance for our human behavior and relationships. Remember, for Jesus there was no theology without ethics and no ethics without theology, for "You shall know a tree by its fruits" (Matthew 7:16).

In Luke, Jesus is pictured responding with the Lord's Prayer to the disciples' request that he teach them to pray (Luke 11:1) and, we may conjecture, they were impressed with how it revived and renewed his spirit. They were impressed, as well, with what an important part prayer had played in the life of "John and his disciples." It is then that Jesus responded with this intensely personal prayer, as Luke presents it, and beginning not with the formal "Our Father in heaven" (Matthew 6:9) but, most assuredly, *"Abba,* hallowed be your name . . ."￼ The same intimate way in which they heard him address God in his own prayers — a familiarity with God that eventually offended the Temple hierarchy who said, as they pointed their fingers, "He calls God his Father!" (John 5:18).

The magnificent thing is that, as the Sermon on the Mount with its Lord's Prayer amply demonstrates, Jesus shares this Parent with us. This is what the Pharisees missed. Jesus, in the final analysis, was not holding his Father to himself but sharing the gracious and parental God with his followers. For, as he said to Mary Magdalene on the morning of his resurrection, "I am ascending to my Father and *your Father,* to my God and your God" (John 20:17).

It is that Parent-God who is seeking to build God's Realm, in part, through us!

Questions For Discussion

1. What does the view that the Lord's Prayer is best understood within the context of a Sermon on the ethics of God's Realm mean to you about its proper use?

2. Is Jesus' teaching more to you than edifying instruction? In what way?

3. What is the difference for you between viewing the Lord's Prayer as a "model" for prayer rather than a ritual prayer?

4. How did Matthew's expanded version of the Lord's Prayer speak to the Early Church's experience of persecution? Would you have found it a personal source of encouragement?

5. Can you describe an occasion when the Lord's Prayer was, for you, the only prayer that "would do"?

Chapter 3

The Realm Of God

Matthew 5:3-10; 6:10, 13; 7:20-21;
Luke 6:20, 22; 6:45-46

The stand-off between the Branch Davidian cult and 400 law enforcement officers in Waco, Texas, lasted for 52 days. Their leader, self-professed messiah David Koresh, believed that the battle of Armageddon was about to begin, a prelude to the Judgment Day and the establishment of the Kingdom of God on earth. For this battle he had armed his followers "to the teeth" with explosives and automatic weapons.

The Branch Davidians are just one example, though an extreme one, of religious groups that have made their narrow interpretation of parts of the New Testament book of Revelation their *magna carta* as they anticipate the instantaneous and supernatural arrival of God's kingdom upon the earth.

It is more than coincidental that this group took the name of David, most celebrated King of Israel, for its title. There is a long history of the Kingdom of God being associated with the empire of David, when Israel was a nation to be reckoned with among the nations of the world, in a **political, militaristic** and **nationalistic** sense!

The eschatological (end times) hope of biblical people is, to be sure, an important element in their world outlook.

Research Activity

See how Jeremiah envisioned the culmination of God's Realm in 11:6 and 2:4. See how Paul identified the Realm of God with the ultimate victory of Christ in Philippians 2:11. How do you envision it? Is such a hope important to you? Why?

The evolution of the Early Church's view of how God's Realm would come is illustrated in the Matthew version of the Lord's Prayer. For a short time God's Realm was identified with the imminent second-coming of Christ. Goods and property were sold and Christians became a waiting community. "Maranatha" or "Come, Lord Jesus" (Revelation 22:20) becomes its **watch** word, and the so-called "Little Apocalypse" (Mark 13:5-31) and the apocalyptic book of Revelation are prominent expressions of that hope in the New Testament.

Mark 13:32-37, the last words of the Little Apocalypse, beginning "but about that day or hour no one knows ... neither the angels nor the Son," and the expanded version of the Lord's Prayer are an important clue to the changing expectation. For to Luke's version, "Thy kingdom come," Matthew adds a clarifying clause, "Thy will be done, on earth as it is in heaven." The emphasis thereby moves from the imminent supernatural arrival of a divine entity, God's Realm, and is more on the establishment of God's rule in every heart — the emphasis of the prophet Jeremiah.

To be sure, the anticipation of sharing in the glory of *Christus Victor* remains, as does the hope that justice and peace will be finally established, but we are satisfied to leave the particulars, including the timing, up to our Parent-God (Mark 13:32b). And we believe that ours is not to be a passive watching, but a diligent watching, as is indeed urged upon us by Jesus in the parables of the Faithful Servant in Matthew 24:45-51 and the Wise and Foolish Virgins in Matthew 25:1-13, where the key phrases are:

> *Blessed is that servant whom his master will find at work when he arrives.* (Matthew 24:46)

> *Keep awake, therefore, for you know neither the day nor the hour.* (Matthew 25:13)

It is important to observe that there is no abandoning of the God's Realm hope but only a reinterpretation. The original hope was one-dimensional: a divine entity superimposed upon creation, with characteristics much like Israel at its peak of success. John of Patmos even speaks of it as "the new Jerusalem" (Revelation 3:12 and 21:2). The later hope is multi-dimensional, including the doing of God's will, the victory of Christ, the expelling of the resistant (Matthew 8:12), the establishment of familial love in the world (Matthew 25:31-46), and eternal life. The "chief end of man — to glorify and enjoy God forever" *(Westminster Shorter Catechism)* will, at last, be achievable!

This Realm, both present and future, is a major theme of Matthew's gospel, and so it is present in both the prologue to the Sermon on the Mount, the Beatitudes, and the epilogue to the Sermon, the Lord's Prayer, and (interestingly enough) is present twice in each of them:

> *Blessed are the poor in spirit, for theirs is the **kingdom of heaven** (5:3) . . . Blessed are those who are persecuted for righteousness' sake, for theirs is the **kingdom of heaven**. (5:10)*

> *Thy **kingdom** come, thy will be done, on earth as it is in heaven (6:10) . . . For Thine is the **kingdom** and the power and the glory forever. Amen. (6:13)*

The Beatitudes speak of God's Realm in the present tense; the Lord's Prayer speaks of God's Realm in both the future (v. 10) and the present (v. 13) tense. Matthew is consistent in its reference to God's Realm as in some aspects in the present and in others in the future. When Jesus is accused by the Pharisees of healing by the power of Beelzebul, he counters, "If I cast out demons by . . . the Spirit of God, then the kingdom of God has come to you" (12:28) — a clear reference to God's Realm as present. When at the Last Supper, Jesus tells the disciples that this is his last meal with them, he adds, "I will drink [wine] new with you in my Father's kingdom" — a clear reference to God's Realm as future. This was apparently a paradox with which Matthew and his Christian contemporaries lived; and it is certainly one, if we are not to amend or revise the gospel account, with which we must live, as well.

To this we need to add that the waning of the hope for an immediate return of Christ and supernatural imposition of the realm of God on earth did not divest the God's Realm hope of its power in the lives of Christians.

Research Activity

Find Jesus' words about the "timing" of God's Realm in Luke 7:20-24. What dimension is emphasized by "within you" as opposed to "upon" or "among" you? Do you experience God's Realm in some way yourself? Explain. Does it bother you that God keeps the "timing" of the fulfillment to Godself?

The natural meaning of the Greek is "within you," and the sense will then be that the Realm of God is experienced now in the hearts of those possessed by Christ's Spirit. Jesus urged his followers to recognize God's sovereignty as a present reality, to be acknowledged by the response of one's total being, love for love — love for the loving God with one's "heart, soul, mind and strength," for one other's neighbor as for oneself (Matthew 22:37-39).

The concept of God's Realm was closely allied with the concept of Messiah. So when John the Baptist's disciples echo John's disillusionment with Jesus, and ask, "Are you he who is to come or shall we look for another?" (Matthew 11:3), Jesus replies:

> *Go and tell John what you hear and see: the blind receive their sight, the lame walk, the lepers are cleansed, the deaf hear, the dead are raised, and the poor have good news [gospel] brought to them.*   (Matthew 11:4-5)

This reply of Jesus' has much in common with the Isaiah passage that Jesus read in the Nazareth Synagogue:

28

The Spirit of the Lord is upon me, because he has anointed me to bring good news to the poor. He has sent me to proclaim release to the captives and recovery of sight to the blind, to let the oppressed go free, to proclaim the acceptable year of the Lord. (Luke 4:18-19)

The Realm of God may be perceived to be present where the Messiah is present with his healing, comforting, liberating compassion and transforming word. This is implicit in many of Jesus' sayings, including, "I am the way, the truth and the life" (John 14:6) and:

Come to me, all you who are weary and heavy-laden, and I will give you rest. Take my yoke upon you and learn of me, for I am gentle and lowly of heart, and you will find rest for your souls. (Matthew 11:28-29)

The understanding that spiritual companionship with the risen Christ is our first experience of God's Realm persists, even as we look forward to a new time in which human hardness of heart shall no longer prevent God's sovereignty from being universal and complete.

Until then, "Behold, he stands at the door and knocks, and if we hear his voice and open the door, he will come in to us and eat with us, and we with him" (Revelation 3:20). Who is there to say that is not an experience of the Realm of God?

Questions For Discussion

1. How does the phrase "Thy will be done on earth as it is in heaven" represent an evolution in early Christians' understanding of how God's Realm comes?

2. How is the concept of God's Realm allied with the concept of the Messiah? (See Matthew 11:4-5 and Luke 4:18-19.)

3. "Realm present" — "Realm future" — which means more to you? Explain. Is this a paradox you can live with?

Chapter 4

A Realm
Above All Kingdoms

Matthew 7:24-27, Luke 6:47-49

> *As Jesus Christ is God's assurance of the forgiveness of all our sins, so ... he is also God's mighty claim upon our whole life .... We reject the false doctrine, as though there were areas of our life in which we would not belong to Jesus Christ, but to other lords .... The Church ... calls to mind the Kingdom of God ... and the responsibility both of rulers and the ruled .... We reject the false doctrine, as though the state, over and beyond its special commission [to provide for justice and peace through reasonable law enforcement] should and could become the single and totalitarian order of human life, thus fulfilling the Church's vocation as well .... The Church's commission ... consists in delivering the message of the free grace of God to all people .... We reject the false doctrine, as though the Church in human arrogance would place the ... work of the Lord in the service of any arbitrarily chosen desires, purposes, and plans.*

So declared representatives of Lutheran, Reformed and United Churches to the Reich (Nazi) Government in May of 1934. They were responding to Hitler's effort to annex the churches under government control through a so-called Party of German Christians. "Let no fear or temptation keep you from treading with us the path of faith and obedience to the Word of God, in order that God's people be of one mind upon earth and that we in faith experience what he himself has said: 'I will never leave you, nor forsake you.'"

It was risky business to defy Hitler in such a way. And, indeed, some of them were imprisoned for their conscientious, though peaceful, resistance. But they knew that to say "Yes" to God's Realm meant saying "No" to the kingdom of the Third Reich.

The situation in the Early Church was no different when the doxological phrases (Matthew 6:13b — RSV footnote) beginning "for thine is the kingdom" were added. Christians were being persecuted for not giving first allegiance to the Roman Emperor. Claudius (A.D. 41-54), Nero (54-68), and Domitian (81-96) persecuted Jews and Christians. The Apostle James, brother of John, was martyred in A.D. 44; James the brother of the Lord in 62, Peter in 64 or 67, and Paul in about 67. Countless Christians were martyred by being burned on crosses or mauled by lions in the Colosseum. It became important to those early believers to reaffirm at every opportunity in their worship together that God's is the Kingdom!

How much and in how many occasions since then the phrase has had the similar meaning for Christians we cannot know. That it can have the same power to encourage in trialsome times is undeniable. Recently I was speaking with the teenage daughter in a Ukranian family of ten who attend the same congregation where I worship. She told me about the attempts to humiliate her as a Christian in the public school of that then Communist state. She was made to stand in front of the class while fellow students wrapped a scarf around her neck and pulled on it in the manner of a gallows, while the rest of the class laughed and jeered. She would come home each day in tears. One Sunday this beautiful girl exhibited the most peaceful expression as she played Ukranian hymns for us on a stringed instrument which she had managed to carry to this land from the land of her birth. It sounded like distant bells. Her face glowed with a peace that can only come from knowing that God's is "the kingdom, the power and the glory."

Rabbi Marvin Schwab of a Sacramento synagogue shares a similar story in the context of the Jewish people's Kingdom meal, the Seder. He reminds us that less than three years ago in the Soviet Union anything printed in Hebrew was illegal and the making of matzo (the unleavened bread of Passover) was outlawed. But as he visited Moscow on a recent Sabbath morning, the section of the Torah that was read contained the "Song of the Sea," the poem in Exodus that recounts how Pharaoh's army was swallowed up by the Sea of Reeds, following the first Passover so long ago.

It came to Rabbi Schwab, as he stood in the pulpit and heard the ancient words of redemption, that he had become a witness to God's Kingdom triumphant again. He brought home a piece of matzo from the factory in St. Petersburg, and he used it at a subsequent Passover Seder. It was, he says, "a Matzo of Hope" — not just for Judaism in Russia but a symbol of hope for pilgrims of God's Realm everywhere.

For Discussion

In our own country, to what kingdoms do we say "No" when we say "Yes" to God's Kingdom? How does our temptation to say "Yes" to other kingdoms show itself? Is it fair to say that no false kingdom is more insidious than the "gospel" that happiness can be bought? Have some popular preachers and television evangelists discovered that by teaching that material prosperity is a sign of God's blessing, they can flourish materially? Can you illustrate?

Former television evangelist Jim Bakker, serving a 45-year prison sentence for misuse of millions of dollars in donations, has had a change of heart in imprisonment. "I have asked God to forgive me and I ask all who have sat under my ministry to forgive me for preaching a gospel emphasizing earthly prosperity," he wrote. He spent several months reading and rereading the words of Jesus, and concluded, "There is no way, if you take the whole counsel of God's word, that you can equate riches or material things as a sign of God's blessing." To the contrary, he observes that Jesus calls his followers to a path often marked by suffering and persecution, even as he promises the Realm of God.

"It is time," he wrote in this remarkable letter from prison, "the call from the pulpit be changed from, 'Who wants a life of pleasure and good things, new homes, cars, material possessions, etc.' to 'Who will come forward to accept Jesus Christ and the fellowship of his suffering?' " We can only hope that this belated insight from Jim Bakker will be contagious for other advocates of a materialistic kingdom.

Research Activity

There are two parables in the Sermon on the Mount. The first is about the disappointed "Lord, Lord" people in Matthew 7:21-23 and the second (Matthew 7:24-27) tells about two houses, one built on sand and one built on a rock. To what might Jesus have been alluding when he spoke of the rock that withstood the stress of wind and flood? To what when he spoke of the one built on sand "and great was its fall"?

Matthew's placement of this parable at the end of the Sermon emphasizes that the teachings of Jesus which have gone before are not for our enjoyment or to be contorted to fit our own brand of gospel, but are, indeed, truths upon which God's Realm is being built! "Great was the fall" is a sobering note upon which to end the Sermon, but it underscores the fact that Jesus saw it as a matter of the utmost urgency that listeners draw these words into the very fiber of their beings! We are challenged to do more than weigh the merit of what is being taught but, indeed, to *become* what we are hearing from Jesus' lips, and to put the imperatives of God's Realm before any other desire or allegiance.

It is said of those first Christians that, despite their experience of repression and persecution, they "were turning the world upside down" (Acts 17:6). That ability to disorient the social order by the consistent promotion and practice of a contrary set of values and aspirations is still possible when we give ourselves to the realm of God.

34

In his book *Kaffir Boy in America*, Mark Mathabane tells of his impressions as a black South African youth visiting this country as a student and tennis athlete. He was almost seduced by material comforts before he observed the superficiality of American "security." Underlying the materialism was a loneliness and insecurity born of anxiety that ill fortune could leave otherwise well-off people destitute and uncared for. Mark came to the conclusion that we should imitate God's preference for the poor and the powerless, enter into God's ongoing activity to liberate people from all that oppresses them and obstructs their development as human beings, and work with God for peace among people. He believes that in God's Realm human life is cherished and all people enjoy creation's many gifts which were created for all.

Where did Mark get a conscience for such ideals? From his Christian mother. "Her simple faith motivated her to invite strangers into our house — drunkards, neurotics, the homeless — to share the scanty meals and crowded shack," he recalls. "She did it," he writes, "because, as she said, 'We're all God's children, and we must take care of each other.' " — Of such is the Realm of God (Matthew 10:14)!

Questions For Discussion

1. How was the situation for German Christians in 1934 similar to that of the Early Church?

2. What is the effect on you of the cultural assumption that material prosperity is a sign of God's blessing?

3. If you had been there when Jesus concluded his Sermon on the Mount with the story about the house built on sand, what would have been your impression?

4. Have you known anyone who "built on a rock," as Mark Mathabane's mother did? What effect has it had on you?

Chapter 5

God's Realm
And God's Power

Matthew 5:3-11, 45; Luke 6:20-22

After Jonah proclaimed what he assumed was a prediction of doom for the people of Nineveh, he sat down outside the city and waited for the disaster to happen. He had come there reluctantly but then found himself relishing the prospect of Nineveh's destruction at the hands of his angry God. But in the course of this remarkable story Jonah was in for disappointment. The king repented in dust and ashes, the people followed his lead, and God spared the city!

It is at that point that Jonah makes a remarkable confession: "I suspected that you were a gracious God all along . . ." (Jonah 4:2b)!

As we finish the story we become aware of a tension in the Bible between an understanding of God as retributive/coercive and one of God as gracious/persuasive. It is a tension that persisted into the time of Jesus and the gospels. It is not a question about God's power, but only of how that power expresses itself.

One cannot read the early books of the Old Testament with any degree of objectivity without observing that the Hebrew people frequently tended to interpret the power of God in terms of the only ruler-model they had — that of the near-eastern potentate: coercive, retributive, self-protecting, even arbitrary. It is an interpretation that prophets like Isaiah, Hosea and Micah, for instance, tried to correct. Recall, for example, Hosea's picture of a God who expresses compassion despite Israel's ingratitude and unresponsiveness:

I led them with cords of human kindness, with bands of love. I was to them like those who lift infants to their cheeks. I bent down to them and fed them.

(Hosea 11:4)

The Psalmist offers an equally passionate defense of the gracious/persuasive understanding of a powerful God:

The Lord is gracious, slow to anger and abounding in steadfast love . . . He does not deal with us according to our sins, nor repay us according to our iniquities . . . as far as the east is from the west, so far he removes our transgressions from us. (Psalm 103:8-12)

"Abounding in steadfast love" — this is the concept of God upon which Jesus centered in his teaching about the parenting nature of God's power. But he did it always against the common traditional understanding of God's power as coercive.

Research Exercise

Review the incident in which the disciples, after an experience of rejection in a Samaritan village, asked Jesus, "Do you want us to command fire to come down from heaven and consume them?" (Luke 9:54). How did Jesus respond? How would you have reacted, given the same situation?

We can understand the early Christians expanding the Lord's Prayer to include a reference to God's *power*, particularly in light of the misuse of power by the Roman emperors to persecute them. It was important to declare to those in power in Rome that God is more powerful, with the implication that God's beleaguered people would ultimately be avenged.

It is imperative for us to recognize that this reference to an all-powerful deity still came within a prayer that begins "Our Father." God's power must be understood within the picture of God as a loving parent. Jesus' numerous appeals for tolerance and forgiveness for one's enemies and reconciliation between adversaries should be adequate correction to the view of God as coercive, retributive and vengeful.

Research Exercise

What did the early Christians' liturgical amendment to the Lord's Prayer, "For Thine is the kingdom and the power . . ." say to Rome? To the Early Church? In what way do you find it personally meaningful?

It is easy to imagine that some Christians in the midst of unjust persecution were thinking, if not outwardly asking, "Who is in charge, anyway?" Perhaps it is partially in response to this concern that Hebrews and Revelation were written. The Hebrews writer reminded them of the faith heroes of yesterday, how their hope was not displaced, and how they were vindicated. He then admonished them to "hold fast to the confession of our hope without wavering, for he who has promised is faithful" (Hebrews 10:23). And the writer of Revelation drew upon Isaiah 35:10, 65:19 and 43:19 to picture a time when "God himself will be with them [and] will wipe away every tear from their eyes, and death and pain will be no more" (Revelation 21:3-4a).

Now, every time they prayed, "Thine is the kingdom and the power and the glory forever," their spirits would be reassured and renewed. God is in charge, and God's power is omnipotent and invincible!

It was left to Jesus to define the nature of God's power as gracious/persuasive rather than retributive/coercive. His teaching about the loving impartiality of God who "marks the sparrow's fall" (Matthew 10:29) and "sends his rain to fall and his sun to shine on the just and unjust" (Matthew 5:45) clearly attests to Jesus' basic understanding of God as gracious/persuasive. And his own ministry and teaching represented the effort of a loving God to persuade God's created children to accept God's gentle rule for their lives. Through Jesus, God invited the children to "love one another as I have loved you" (John 15:12).

There is an implied description of the gracious/persuasive God in Paul's First Letter to the Corinthians, the much-admired 13th chapter. Paul is urging us there to reflect the characteristics of God:

> ... *patient and kind, not envious or boastful, not arrogant or rude ... not irritable or resentful, does not rejoice at wrong-doing, but rejoices in the truth. There is no limit to [God's] endurance, no end to [God's] trust, no fading of [God's] hope; it can outlast anything. It is, in fact the one thing that still stands when all else has fallen.* (1 Corinthians 13:4-8 JBP)[1]

One of the best pictures of the gracious/persuasive God is to be found in the otherwise fiery apocalypse of John of Patmos, as part of the Seven Letters to the Churches that are in Asia:

> *Listen! I am standing at the door, knocking; if you hear my voice and open the door, I will come in to you and eat with you, and you with me.*
> (Revelation 3:20 NRSV)

Perhaps we are ready now to define the character of God's power. And, unfortunately, we do it within the context of today's concepts of power, which weigh it heavily in the direction of coercive power. Military superiority constitutes national power, dominating and belittling one's opponents constitutes political power, having more than one's share of the world's goods constitutes economic power, and competing successfully with one's peers for recognition and material wealth implies personal power!

In stark contrast, the teachings of Jesus emphasize mercy and justice, service and sacrifice, humility and simplicity, sharing and a conciliatory spirit — in his day as counter-culture and ethically radical as they are today! The Beatitudes make no sense at all if one buys society's definitions of power. But they make all the sense in the world if we understand God's power to be *the power of love!*

Henri Nouwen, contemplating Rembrandt's *Return of the Prodigal Son*, speaks for many of us when he writes:

> *Here is the God I want to believe in: a Father who, from the beginning of creation, has stretched out his arms in merciful blessing, never forcing himself on anyone, but always waiting; never letting his arms drop down in despair, but always hoping that his children will return so that he can speak words of love to them and let his tired arms rest on their shoulders.* [2]

The understanding of God's power as retributive/coercive came to a cataclysmic conclusion when self-proclaimed messiah, David Koresh, after 52 days resisting federal officers' demands that he surrender himself and 85 adherents of the Branch Davidian cult, reputedly ordered the compound to be burned to the ground with everyone, including women and children, inside. "Don't move until you see God," he told his followers. Koresh apparently thought that his God would want them to die in a conflagration — his version of Armageddon. Only a handful survived. The understanding of God as gracious/persuasive was lost in the urgent need to view God as retributive/coercive.

How could God be patient with a vacillating, idolatry-prone Israel? How could Jesus be patient with an uncomprehending religious establishment? How can the Lord be patient with a society that mouths his name while it ignores his teachings? God can be patient because God's is the power of love, not of coercion.

Research Activity

The inexplicable patience of God with a fickle and wayward people is the theme of Hosea. Look up Hosea 11:8-9. Do you welcome Hosea's portrayal of God as gracious/persuasive? What significance does this have for you personally?

In the Hosea passage above God specifically disassociates Godself from humankind's use of power for revenge, control or domination. God, for better or for worse, casts God's lot with persuasive rather than coercive power. God's is the power of love!

Knowing this and, further, having defined it in the caring and sacrificial ministry of Jesus, John, in his First Epistle, makes the most sweeping definition of God's nature as grace that scripture can offer:

> *Whoever does not love does not know God, for God is love .... By this we know that we abide in God and God with us, because God has given us of his Spirit .... There is no fear in love, but perfect love casts out fear .... We love because God first loved us.*
>
> (1 John 4:8, 13, 18-19)

Questions For Discussion

1. Have you noticed the tension in the Bible between an understanding of God as retributive/coercive and one of God as gracious/persuasive? How have you tried to resolve the apparent contradiction for your own understanding?

2. With which understanding of God does Jesus appear to be siding? Does a parent's being gracious/persuasive exclude "tough love"? What was your experience as a child?

3. Is it fair to say that today's concept of power leans heavily in the direction of coercive power? What are the implications for you, a Christian, as you seek to model Jesus in your life and work?

1. J. B. Phillips, *The New Testament In Modern English*, (New York: MacMillan & Sons, c. 1958, 1959), p. 361

2. *Weavings,* July-August, 1993, p. 31.

Chapter 6

God's Realm And God's Glory

Matthew 6:1-18, 7:15

To the "What is the chief end of man?" question of the *Westminster Shorter Catechism* of 1647, the Westminster divines answered: "The chief end of man is to glorify God and enjoy him forever." These enthusiastic Reformers were still reacting to other hierarchies that were demanding glory: royal and ecclesiastical sovereigns, and an entrenched nobility. In saying God's is "the glory" they were rejecting competing claims for glory from human institutions, personages and classes.

When Luke wrote of the birth of Jesus in Bethlehem, he envisioned a "host of angels singing, 'Glory to God in the highest ...' " (2:13-14).

When John of Patmos envisioned a hymn to God suitable for the victory celebration in the restored creation, he wrote:

> *Hallelujah! Salvation and glory and power to our God, for his judgments are true and just .... Praise to our God, all you his servants, and all who fear him, both small and great .... Let us rejoice and exult and give him the glory, for the marriage of the lamb has come, and his bride [church] has made herself ready ....*
>
> (Revelation 19:1-7)

When the early Christians enhanced the Lord's Prayer by adding a doxological conclusion, "For Thine is the kingdom and the power and the glory forever," they emphasized that, as with power and realm, God's glory is for God alone, a tribute to be given only to God.

43

An interesting thing about this word *glory* is its dual usage. Above it is used synonymously with *praise*. But because the praise being called for here is praise for God, unlike any other kind of praise — parent for child, teacher for student, spouse for spouse, etc. — there has to be another word that may be used only in reference to God, and the word is glory. The other use of glory is illustrated especially well in the Revelation passage given above. Here we are called to join the saints in singing of the glory — the radiance, the shimmering aura that emanates from God — and to give God glory (i.e. praise).

In the Bible the image of darkness, recalling the dark primeval chaos of the earth before the creative hand of God brought light and form and order, stands for all in the world that attempts to pull us back to chaos and away from the purposeful movement toward God's Kingdom of unity and peace. When Jesus endeavored to picture what it is like not to be included among the dinner guests in the Kingdom of Heaven, he used the image of darkness:

> *The [erstwhile] heirs of the kingdom will be thrown into*
> *the outer darkness.*　　　　　(Matthew 8:12)

If there is a state or a place where the presence of God cannot be perceived or enjoyed, it is this place of outer darkness. Jesus made the same reference in the Parable of the Wedding Banquet (Matthew 22:1-14). There outer darkness is where there are pathetic gestures of regret — "weeping and gnashing of teeth" — and is the fate of the first invited who made excuses.

Rabbi Harold Kushner appropriates this biblical image effectively as an explanation for the presence of evil in the world, supposing that there were some pockets of primeval chaos, corners of the world, where God's creative light did not reach. These pockets of darkness are always at work attempting to pull humankind and creation back to chaos. For him, this explains the presence of evil in the world.

John draws upon these understandings in the Prologue to his Gospel:

*He was in the beginning with God. All things came into being through him . . . . What has come into being in him was life, and the life was the light of all people. The light shines in **the darkness**, and the darkness, did not overcome it . . . . The true light which enlightens everyone, was coming into the world . . . and we have seen his **glory**, the glory as of a father's only son, full of grace and truth . . . From his fullness we have all received, grace upon grace.*   (John 1:2-16 NRSV)

John sees Jesus emanating from God as creative light, and coming into the world to dispel the darkness and complete God's creative work. In John, Jesus says, "I am the light of the world. Whoever follows me shall have the light of life . . . this is the judgment, that the light has come into the world, and people loved darkness rather than light because their deeds were evil" (John 8:12 and 3:19).

Dr. Martin E. Marty has observed how the collapse of the communist bloc and the lifting of repressive controls on dismembered states has unleashed latent ethnic/religious friction and conflicts. He concludes that this is only one sign of the antagonisms that are interrupting a movement of the world to more inclusive unity. Just when we are moving to concepts stressing the interconnectedness of the world and the human family, religious and ethnic zealotry is pushing the world out to the margins, the edges. In that chaos, those who won't tolerate diversity or compromise are formidable aggressors!

For Discussion
In what areas of the nation and world is religious-linked discord and conflict distressingly apparent? Do you share Dr. Marty's alarm? Do you agree that forces are pushing the world from a movement toward global community to global fracturing? What would be the greatest loss?

Marty concludes that there is little we can do to prevent the worst from happening. But I firmly believe that we may find encouragement in John's words, "The true light has come into the world, and the darkness has not overcome it" (John 1:5).

Into such a situation the teacher of the Sermon on the Mount's voice may yet be heard, blessing peacemakers and urging children of God to take the initiative in reconciliation with acts of forgiveness, service, and generosity. He calls us to be like leaven, good salt and light to the world. An early baptismal charge catches the spirit of the Sermon:

> *Go into the world in peace; be of good courage; hold fast to that which is good. Render to no one evil for evil. Strengthen the fainthearted; support the weak; heal the afflicted. Honor everyone, rejoicing in God and the power of the Holy Spirit.*

In other words, we are asked to help God in the task of dispelling chaos and enlarging the dominion of God's light, in bringing to completion God's peaceable realm.

For Discussion

How in their doxological ending to the Lord's Prayer were the early Christians affirming that the darkness they were experiencing in a hostile world would not overcome the progress of God's glory (light) in the world? Do you think they despaired over the ruthless Imperial effort to exterminate or neutralize the fellowship of believers? Why? Why not?

The early Christians were, it seems, affirming at every opportunity that God only is worthy, ultimately, of human praise. With the psalmist, they saw human praise of God as on a continuum with the daily praise that the created order gives to the Creator:

> *Let the heavens be glad, and let the earth rejoice; let the sea roar, and all that fills it; let the field exult, and everything*

in it. Then shall all of the trees of the forest sing for joy
before the Lord. (Psalm 96:11-13)

In "the Lord's answer to Job" we are again carried back
to the creation story and the glory given to God by creation:

. . . when I laid the foundation of the earth . . . when the
morning stars sang together, and all the heavenly beings
shouted for joy. (Job 38:4, 7)

Worshippers do not see themselves as originators of praise
but as those who join in praise already begun in heaven and
in the created order. As praise of God is "natural" for the
rest of God's world, so it should be for us, they reasoned.

Come, let us sing to the Lord; let us make a joyful noise
to the rock of our salvation! Let us come into his presence
with thanksgiving; let us make a joyful noise to him with
songs of praise. (Psalm 95:1-2)

I have observed a remarkable phenomenon at ecumenical
gatherings. Those who might otherwise participate defensive-
ly or dutifully in discussions of doctrine or church practices,
or be uncomfortable with the trappings or ritual of denomi-
nations not their own, drop their defensiveness and critical demeanor when they join in singing glory to God. As they raise
their voice in praise to God, the distinctions that separate them
are, at least momentarily, forgotten. Their faces become bright
and their spirits joyous in the singing of simple songs of praise.
For that time, at least, giving glory to God together becomes
the most natural and spontaneous thing they can do.

That must be a preview of life in the heavenly kingdom.
It certainly is the best picture that the John of Revelation can
possibly offer. John pictures the citizens of the New Jerusalem being called to praise:

Praise our God, all you his servants,
and all who fear him, small and great.
(Revelation 19:5)

47

And the multitude of voices ring out in thunderous acclaim:

> *Hallelujah! For the Lord our God the Almighty reigns.*
> *Let us rejoice and exult and give him the glory ...*
> (Revelation 19:6-7a)

The early Christians trying to be united and strong in the face of demands for their ultimate allegiance from Rome were a diverse lot. They came from all over the Roman world: Jews and Gentiles, nobility and servant class, educated and uneducated, rich and poor. We can be sure that a principal element of their unity was their common need to give glory to God together, with every knee bowing and every tongue confessing "that Christ is Lord, to the glory of God the Father" (Philippians 2:11).

Jesus warns in the Sermon on the Mount that there will be those seeking glory that belongs to God alone: those who "sound trumpets before" them when they give alms, those who make great show when they pray, those who parade their fasting with exaggerated humility, those who gather treasures unto themselves, those who feign love for God even as they worship material prosperity, those who judge others from a posture of moral superiority, and those "who come in sheep's clothing but inwardly are ravenous wolves" (Matthew 7:15).

The tragic aspect of this picture that Jesus draws is that it is of the very people who are called to give glory to God and the ones most tempted to seek glory for themselves!

Recalling regularly, then, the phrase of the Lord's Prayer, "Thine is the glory," can be an important corrective for us. The Christian who seeks glory, the church that seeks glory, the pastor who seeks glory, and the so-called Christian nation that seeks glory will not be at home in the Realm of God. For there there is only One to whom belongs honor and glory: God, who wears divine glory as a crown! Hallelujah! Amen.

48

Questions For Discussion

1. What are the two ways "glory" is used in the Bible?

2. How important is the image of darkness versus light in scripture? Is this a hopeless conflict? What word of hope does John give in the prologue to his gospel?

3. What challenge does the world's movement from inclusive unity to global fracturing, as Dr. Marty describes it, present to those committed to reconciliation and peace-making?

Part 2

Our Part In
The Realm Of God

Chapter 7

Trusting
Our Parent-God

Matthew 5:45-47, 7:9-11, Luke 6:35-36

If we were compelled to hold up just one feature of the Sermon on the Mount as distinguishing and unprecedented in a biblical sense, it would have to be Jesus' almost exclusive use of the term *Father* for God.

It was on this characteristic of his teaching that the Jewish hierarchy pounced as they began to accuse him of blasphemy and unorthodox teaching. "He calls God his own father, therefore making himself equal to God!" (John 5:18).

To this accusation Jesus gave a surprising and confounding response. His referring to God as Father was a sign of humility not of self-exaltation. "I can do nothing on my own. As I hear, I judge; and my judgment is just, because I seek to do not my own will but the will of him who sent me" (John 5:30).

This natural way of calling God *Father* had an opposite effect upon the common people. They had heard God called Father before in religious teaching, but invariably as an assertion that God created the human race, as in Malachi 2:10, "Have we not all one father? Has not one God created us?" Now the hints of God's parental affection that were to be found in Isaiah, Jeremiah, Hosea and the Psalms fairly blossomed in the teaching and prayers of Jesus!

If the record of Luke is to be accepted, Jesus' understanding of God as his Father, in a warm, real and dynamic sense, appeared as early as his bar mitzvah in Jerusalem at age 12, "Did you not know that I must be in my Father's house?" (Luke 2:49).

By the time Jesus was driven by the Spirit into the wilderness "to be tempted by the accuser" (Matthew 4:1) at approximately age 30, and there to struggle with goals and strategy as he who was "anointed to bring good news to the poor" (Luke 4:18), his understanding of himself as God's Son was firmly fixed. For the temptations came to him in that context: "If you are the Son of God ..." (Matthew 4:3-6). At the end of that conflict it was that parent-God whom Matthew pictures coming, through angels, to "wait on him" (Matthew 4:11).

But even more unique to Jesus was the frequent use of a common Aramaic word *Abba* in addressing God! Abba was most often used by children in addressing their natural fathers. There is no indication that, aside from Jesus, it was ever used in addressing or speaking of God. An English equivalent might be Papa.

Research Activity
    Find "Father" in a Bible Dictionary, noting comments on the use of Abba by Jesus and by Paul. What is *unique* about Abba as opposed to, simply, Father?

So distinctive was Jesus' use of Abba that Mark and Paul use it in that Aramaic form in their otherwise Greek writings! Paul makes important implications from Jesus' use of Abba: "When we cry 'Abba! Father' it is the Spirit bearing witness with our spirit that we are children of God ... joint heirs with Christ" (Romans 8:15-17).

Once we grasp Jesus' understanding and experience of God as our Papa — as caring, protective and nurturing as the best human parent might be, and more so — then the assurances of the Sermon on the Mount take on new reality and vividness! For in the Sermon, the Teacher who begins his model prayer with "Our Father" tells us that the God who feeds the birds of the air and clothes the lilies of the field counts us as more valuable, understands our needs, and will provide what we need (Matthew 6:25-33).

Jesus' bread and stone analogy in 7:9-11 makes the point even more clearly:

Is there any among you who, if your child asks for bread, will give him a stone? Or if a child asks for a fish, will give him a snake? If you then, who are evil, know how to give gifts to your children, how much more will your heavenly Father give good things to those who ask him?

Furthermore, Jesus says that God dispenses nature's gifts impartially:

Your Father in heaven makes the sun to shine on the evil and the good, and sends rain on the righteous and the unrighteous. (Matthew 5:45)

This, in contrast to the teachers of the law who count some people unworthy of their ministries or God's consideration. They scoffed at Jesus because he ate "with tax collectors and sinners" (Matthew 9:11).

But lest some of his hearers forget that the generous God is also a God who desires right living from God's children, Jesus calls upon them to "be perfect ... as your heavenly Father is perfect" (Matthew 5:48), an imperative that has caused no end of frustration and guilt.

Let me try to put this saying in context. It immediately follows the above testimony to God's impartiality with nature's gifts in 5:45, and Jesus' admonition against our being choosey with *our* gifts:

If you love those who love you, what reward do you have ... And if you greet only your brothers and sisters, what more are you doing than others? (Matthew 5:46-47)

The perfection of God, says Jesus, is God's grace, God's impartiality. When we are the same with *our* gifts, God is pleased. When we are selective and show partiality with our gifts, our heavenly Parent is disappointed. This contrasts greatly with the "perfection" touted by the pious elite of Jesus' day, who wore long fringe on their garments as a sign of their moral perfection but who "neglect the weightier matters of the law: justice, mercy and faith" (Matthew 23:23).

Too often we define this admonition of Jesus in moralistic terms (i.e. adherence to rules), whereas Jesus was speaking of the caring and impartial sharing of our natural gifts, expressions of goodwill between God's children. Jesus is right: sharing *is* an expression of which all who understand themselves and others to be children of God are capable.

One of the most memorable aspects of Bonhoeffer's account of his Nazi imprisonment is his description of how he would consciously decide each morning to greet his guards in a positive way. As a result of his refusal to dehumanize them in his thinking as they sometimes did with him, Bonhoeffer was able to have a positive effect on several of them. They grieved, along with his friends, when he was executed.

For Discussion
What "more" is Jesus asking from you and me when he says, "If you love and greet only those who love you, your brothers and sisters, what reward have you, and what more are you doing than others" (Matthew 5:47)? What kind of love limits had he observed with them? With what kind of love limits might Jesus challenge you?

Why Matthew's emphasis on *heavenly* or *in heaven* with the name *Father?* What dimension does this add? It means, certainly, more than simply the habitat of God. It is making a statement about the supremacy, the sovereignty, and the invincibility of God. Because God the Parent is "above all" (John 3:31) we, as we receive God's promises and reach for the life and relationships that are pleasing to God, can be certain that nothing above God will defeat or overrule God. God's hopes and dreams for us may be frustrated temporarily but they will never be abolished or annulled, for these values, these principles, and this love foundation are *built into* the universe by the Sovereign of the universe. Hence, the Apostle Paul could rhapsodize: "Faith, hope, love *abide* . . . and the greatest of these is *love*" (1 Corinthians 13:13)!

Earlier we observed that the version of the Lord's Prayer that we find in Matthew, in contrast with the much simpler version in Luke, may be a product of the worshipping community, the Early Church. The length is not the only clue. The Prayer begins with *Our*. This Prayer is, from the first word, a corporate prayer. There are two aspects of *Our* that were particularly relevant for a confessing community under siege from political and religious powers: a community whose original hopes for the immediate return of Christ and the simultaneous emergence of God's Realm were fading.

The first aspect of *Our* is that defined in 1 Peter 2:9-10:

> *You are a chosen race, a royal priesthood, a holy nation, God's **own people**, in order that you may proclaim the mighty acts of him who called you out of darkness into his marvelous light. Once you were not a people, but now you are **God's people** . . .*

God who was *in heaven* — Sovereign, above all, eternal — would not "leave or forsake" them (Hebrews 13:5). They were chosen, called out, and the One who called them would not abandon them nor disappear but would be with them always — loyal and invincible! *Our* implied the assurance that the God who called them out would stick with them through thick and thin!

The other aspect of *Our* that reassured those first Christians was the implication of their commitment to one another. Not *my* God but *ours*. They were committed to support, encourage and cherish one another as members of the same body. This attitude is best illustrated in Paul's description in 1 Corinthians 12:25-26:

> *. . . no dissension within the body, but members having the same care for one another. If one member suffers, all suffer together . . . if one member is honored, all rejoice together . . .*

The Lord's Prayer begins with an affirmation of the invincible God's parental commitment to them and of their unwavering commitment to one another. They knew, that even in that kind of world, this was an unbeatable combination!

Questions For Discussion

1. How important is it to you that Jesus called God "Father"?

2. How did Jesus' understanding of God as Father set the tone for the Sermon on the Mount?

3. What do you think Jesus is saying to you when he commands, "You must be perfect as your heavenly Father is perfect" (Matthew 5:48)?

4. What dimension did "in heaven" add to the Early Church's understanding of God? What meaning does it have for you?

5. What does the "our" before Father mean to you? What does it imply about your relationship with other Christians?

Chapter 8

People Of
Honesty And Integrity

Matthew 5:33-37

What was it that caused the phrase "Hallowed be Thy name" (Matthew 6:9) to be added to Jesus' simple prayer as recorded in Luke 11:2-4? What was it in the life and experience of the early believers that gave them a concern about how God's name was used?

To be sure, the concern about the use of sacred vocabulary in the making of oaths or as witness to the truth of one's statements or promises was present in Jesus' teachings:

> *Again, you have heard that it was said to those of ancient times, "You shall not swear falsely, but carry out the vows you have made to the Lord." But I say to you, Do not swear at all, either by heaven, for it is the throne of God, or by the earth, for it is his footstool, or by Jerusalem, for it is the city of the great King. And do not swear by your head, for you cannot make one hair white or black. Let your word be "Yes, Yes" or "No, No"; anything more than this comes from the evil one.*
> (Matthew 5:33-37)

> *Woe to you, blind guides, who say, "Whoever swears by the sanctuary is bound by nothing, but whoever swears by the gold of the sanctuary is bound by the oath." You blind fools! For which is greater, the gold or the sanctuary that has made the gold sacred? And you say, "Whoever swears by the altar is bound by nothing, but whoever swears by the gift on the altar is bound by the oath." How blind you are! For which is greater, the gift or the altar that makes the gift sacred? So whoever swears by the altar swears by everything on it, and whoever*

swears by the sanctuary, swears by it and the One who dwells in it; and whoever swears by heaven, swears by the throne of God and by the One who is seated upon it.
(Matthew 23:16-22)

In the later saying Jesus is making reference to the Pharisees' voluminous interpretation of the Law, the Midrash, as he does in Mark 7:13, where he accuses the Pharisees and scribes with "making void the word of God through [their] tradition that [they] have handed on." Jesus does not reject the Law. In the Sermon he specifically states that he has come "not to abolish the law or the prophets . . . but to fulfill" (Matthew 5:17). But he does reject the Midrash which the teachers used as if it were the Torah, the five books of the law: Genesis through Deuteronomy.

The Midrash is full of subtle distinctions between what is and what is not permissible in practicing the biblical laws, some of them so outrageously picky and illogical that they would be funny, were it not for the despair that they caused common people who really wanted to please God with their behavior. Jesus saw it as just another attempt by the legalists to intimidate the common people and make pretense to their own exclusive righteousness!

On the other hand, Jesus saw many merchants, cheats and plagiarists taking advantage of the fine distinctions made by the Midrash. Following the lead of the Pharisees' interpretation, they would carefully phrase impressive oaths and promises so that the customer, client or court would be convinced of their good faith while they were literally clear of breaking the law of God. So common was this practice that no one knew whom to believe!

Jesus effectively warns his listeners not to make sacred oaths at all but to develop such a reputation for honesty that people understand them to be as good as their word: "Let your word be 'Yes, Yes,' or 'No, No.' More than this comes from [is flirting with] evil" (Matthew 5:37).

There are two ways to use the Lord's name that Jesus models in the Sermon on the Mount: in prayer, and in teaching about God. And the name for God which Jesus prefers is *Father*. And we know why. Because it says to the common people that we owe our creation to God, and that we can count on God to deal with us as a good parent would! The name Father — or, speaking inclusively, Parent — elicits thoughts of both discipline and unconditional love, characteristics richly illustrated in the Sermon.

Research Activity

In Exodus 20:1-17 with which of the Ten Commandments can Jesus' teaching about a proper use of God's name be associated? What do you think was the concern at the time that Moses presented the Decalogue? What was the problem at the time Jesus made his statements (above)? What are ways God's name or religious language is used pretentiously or with ulterior motives today?

Super-salesmen and con artists today are apt to manipulate through communication techniques and psychological ploys. They know what buttons to push on people: greed, ambition, lust, rivalry, guilt, sensuality, self-indulgence, materialism, vanity. Divine names may not be used, but the same motivation to deceive, confuse or entice are present, and that makes us as liable to the judgment of God as does blasphemy. For God, as Jesus makes clear, is interested in relationships of honesty, empathy and kindness with the goal of serving, not using, the other person.

Some of us are becoming aware in the political arena today of a more glaring kind of blasphemy. It is the use of God's name and so-called biblical teachings to push a particular political agenda or to court conservative Christian voters. Some ambitious politicians with little or no personal Christian allegiance, but who are impressed with the political clout of conservative Christian political activists, are using the language in order to court their favor!

Yes, high-sounding patriotic and religious language, like the kissing of babies, is an old ploy to court voters. But there is, besides the sheer deceit involved, another hazard to such a strategy. Rhetoric full of references to God, Christian family values and Christian nation spoken in sectarian language can further fracture our already badly divided society, and undermine our constitutional guarantee that each citizen may practice religion or not in his or her own way. It does not please God that God's hallowed name is used in order to manipulate people or isolate those not of our persuasion, no matter how noble our intentions.

To return to an early question of this chapter, the concern of the Early Church about the use of God's name was surely motivated in a large part by the persecution they were experiencing. The Emperor of Rome was asking them to share God's hallowed name with himself, and thus to accept a multiplicity of gods. There were surely some church people who were tempted to make this "one small" compromise in order to avoid torture or death. It was only, after all, a matter of a few words spoken compliantly in a brief moment. Many others of them knew that this compromise would be the first of many; that "the beast" is never satisfied. They understood also that to refuse to comply would be a way of testifying to the one and only God and Father of their Lord, Jesus Christ. The One who accepted a cross in order not to let go of them was asking them to share his "cup" out of love for God and one another. This was one of the meanings that "Hallowed be Thy name" had for first century Christians.

It had another significance, as well. As the early church called their members to divest themselves of worldly goods and enter into a covenant of communal life as they awaited the imminent second coming of Christ, some took the vow with their "fingers crossed."

Research Activity

Look up Acts 5:1-11. How did Ananias and Saphira try to deceive their brothers and sisters with regard to some land they had sold? How might their deed have violated a vow they had made to the Christian community of which they were a part?

Perhaps out of humiliation when they were confronted by the Apostles, they dropped dead and were carried from the meeting place. We can be sure that none who witnessed this would ever take vows in God's name lightly again. Luke comments, "Great fear seized the whole church and all who heard of these things" (Acts 5:11).

This seems like a bizarre instance to us — nothing like it in the rest of the New Testament. But its presence in the record points up to us the seriousness with which the Bible takes the issue of vows in God's name. God's name is "hallowed" — valued, holy, revered. It is never to be used as a deception, a ploy, a manipulation or in pretense.

How is God's name to be used? As Jesus used it: to tell others, joyfully, gratefully about God, to sing God's praises, and to pray to God:

O give thanks to the Lord, call on his name,
Make known his deeds among the peoples.
Sing to him . . . tell of his wonderful works.
Glory in his holy name; let the hearts of those who seek
the Lord rejoice!

(Psalm 105:1-3)

Questions For Discussion

1. What was the major factor in the experience of the Early Church explaining its concern for how God's name was used and honored?

2. Why did Jesus reject the Pharisees' Midrash even while he respected the Law of Moses?

3. What does Jesus suggest as an alternative to making grand-sounding oaths? (See Matthew 5:37.)

Chapter 9

Living Simply
As A Means To Sharing

Matthew 6:25-33, Luke 12:22-31

In a short essay written for a newspaper-sponsored writing contest on the theme "I'd like to explore . . . ," prize-winner Karen Brewer said:

> *I have never gone to bed hungry. I have never fallen asleep wondering if I will live to see morning. I have never awakened to the sound of shouts and gunfire . . . What do Somali children feel when a parent or sibling dies? Pain and anger at a cruel world? Or inner peace, knowing that their loved ones have been taken from tremendous suffering to a quiet end? . . . Where do they gain the strength to continue living when those close to them die? How can they be strong, surrounded by such suffering? Do they look to the future with hope for a better life? Or have they quietly accepted the futility of their situation? How do Somali children endure in an environment which has forced them to grow up too fast?*

How does an American teenager from an affluent neighborhood become so sensitive to the basic needs of children on the other side of the world?

There is a new awareness that we cannot continue to live so self-indulgently while most of the world goes hungry. If one member of a family of 20 eats nearly a quarter of the loaf, it is easy to see that some of the remaining members will go to bed hungry.

Jesus, in his model prayer, makes it clear that members of the human family are called to a life of simplicity when it comes to basic needs: "Give us this day our daily bread" (Matthew 6:11), not as an ascetic exercise designed to test one's "spirituality," but as a way to see that the basic needs of every member of the human family are met.

It would not be the only time that Jesus would stress the need for each one to keep his or her own wants minimal. When he sent out 70 disciples to pass the peace and announce the breaking-in kingdom of God, he instructed them not to carry purse, bag or sandals, relying on the good will of those who welcomed them to be fed and sheltered (Luke 10:1-12).

Further he cautioned against wealth and abundance: "It is hard for a rich man to enter the kingdom" (Matthew 19:23). "Woe to him who stores up treasures for himself but is not rich toward God" (the Parable of the Rich Fool, Luke 12:16-21). And he told of a rich man who would not share the crumbs from his table with the dying poor man at his door and ended up in Hades, tormented mostly by the thought that his rich brothers may not learn the lesson he has learned until it is too late (Luke 16:19-31).

The *daily bread* petition of the Lord's Prayer logically follows the admonitions toward simple needs and trustful living which abound in the Sermon on the Mount.

Research Activity

Look up Matthew 6:25-33 (Jesus' words about anxiety and insecurity related to the daily necessities of life). What is Jesus saying about our Creator's oversight? How many times does Jesus use "worry" or "worrying"? Is there a human tendency to doubt that there will ever be "enough" to meet our physical needs? What does it mean to "strive first for the kingdom of God"?

The practical wisdom of Jesus' advocacy of a simple lifestyle may be finally coming into light for us. Admittedly, it has come more from concerns for dwindling resources, exhausted landfill, toxic waste disposal, and dependence on foreign oil than from respect for Jesus' teachings. Nevertheless, average people are taking more seriously than ever the option of a simpler lifestyle and trimming down their list of "needs."

Deterrent to serious consideration of such a gentle and respectful way of living is the paralysis of the realization that we may never be able to live like Saint Francis or Mother Teresa. But many are seeing that they can move little by little. Tony Campolo of Eastern College said in an interview for *Marriage Partnership* magazine: "I believe that God cheers us as we move rather than condemning us for not being where we ought to be. I believe he accepts us where we are and leads us into the future."

It is often assumed by government economists that the reason for an economic recession is a lack of consumer confidence. But what if we land in a recession because Americans stop buying what they don't need? The federal government's answer has been to give the middle class more money so that they can spend more, to increase their "buying power." We have been told to "spend, spend, spend," and increasingly we are answering, "But I don't need anything." We look forward to leadership in Washington that will not say, "Spend anyway." If they continue to do so, students of the Sermon on the Mount are obligated to say, "Enough!"

Dietrich Bonhoeffer, in his exegesis of the Beatitudes, *The Cost of Discipleship,* makes it clear that the phrase "blessed are the poor" refers to those who have chosen to become poor. The people in Haiti, for example, who are impoverished through no choice of their own, are not necessarily the *blessed,* despite their suffering. The blessed are those who choose to unpackage their lives and live more simply.

Research Activity

John Wesley once said, "It is the obligation of every Christian to work as hard as he can to make as much money as he can to spend as little as he can in order to give as much as he can." In what way is the question, "How much is enough?" a very personal and individual question? Why must we be careful about imposing our answers on other people? Do you agree that living with simplicity of needs as Jesus urges it upon us is desirable? What kind of commitment does it require?

When we do choose to unpackage our lives and live more simply that others might "simply live," many other things will fall into proper perspective. Material things are expendable, perishable, temporal ("moth and rust corrupt and thieves break in and steal" — Matthew 6:19). Lives saved or revived even partially as a result of our sharing is an occurrence whose reverberations, like the "stone in the pond," never stop (Treasure in heaven, which does not rot or rust and cannot be stolen — Matthew 6:20).

But as the Shaker song says:

> *'Tis a gift to be simple*
> *'Tis a gift to be free*
> *'Tis a gift to come down*
> *Where you ought to be.*

Those who come to the place where they consciously choose to have less so that others might have a better chance at qualitative life will not congratulate themselves for having done so, nor will they have gotten there because someone presented them with enough valid rational arguments. They will have gotten there because God gave them eyes to see the shallowness of their self-indulgence and the suffering of God's other children.

On a family trip to Mexico City several years ago, our ten-year-old daughter, through the train window, watched children on the outskirts of the city, scrambling up dirt piles between their hovels of cardboard and scrap metal. "People don't really live there, do they?" she asked. Her expression of wonder turned to sadness as we answered, "Yes, Nancy, I'm afraid they do." The memory of those slums has haunted her through the years in a good way that has increased her sensitivity toward others and made her reflect on the kind of lifestyle she should embrace. Now, as she helps a church develop a pre-school, she is asking them to program into it scholarships for poor children at a ratio of one to nine — to include children whose single parent must work just to keep food on the table. "The others can carry them," she says.

Perhaps parents should make sure their families with children age ten or more spend at least part of their yearly vacation in a less privileged environment at a Christian center in the inner city, at an orphanage south of the border, or helping a neighborhood center with a summer recreational program.

Jesus had empathy for poor people and people with problems because he spent time with them. And, because of his own simple lifestyle they were not "put off" by him.

To narrow down the whole possible spectrum of material requests to "our daily bread" is to make a conscious choice to live simply so that others might simply live. It has nothing to do with adopting a simple lifestyle as a badge of spirituality, saying, "Look how worn my clothes are, how lousy my car is. Am I a super saint or what?" Those are the people who say, "Wait a minute, Lord, didn't we do so many admirable things in your name?" but who discover that Jesus never got to know them (Sermon on the Mount, Matthew 7:21-23).

No, it is more like those whose sharing spirit was so spontaneous that they lost track of the things they had done, and responded to Jesus' commendation with, "But Lord, when did we see thee hungry and feed thee or thirsty and give thee drink?" to which Jesus responded, "Insofar as you did it unto one of the least of these . . . you did it to me" (Matthew 25:37, 40).

Questions For Discussion

1. Do you agree that more and more people are waking up to the fact that we cannot live so self-indulgently while most of the rest of the world goes hungry?

2. Do you agree that the prayer petition, "Give us this day our daily bread," calls us, in part, to a life of simplicity in terms of our basic needs?

3. What value might it be for a fairly privileged family to spend some time among the poor?

Chapter 10

Forgiven Forgivers

Matthew 5:21-48, Luke 6:27-36

It was a gathering that no one could have ever envisioned. The adult sons and daughters of extermination camp survivors and Nazi camp officers sitting in a room together discussing the feelings that had plagued them since childhood! There was the inevitable outpouring of anger and grief. The children of the camp survivors saw the numbers tattooed on their parents' wrists and they heard the terrible stories of separation, torment and death. They told how the shadow of their parents' hideous experience cast its pall upon them, as well. They confessed the feelings, apprehension, even revulsion, that came over them as they anticipated the meeting with their German counterparts.

The adult children of the Nazi officers spoke of similar feelings. They too, in childhood, had experienced the spectres hanging over them — the terrible conflict between love for their parents and confusion and revulsion at what had happened in the camps. In some ways, they carried the same guilt and regret that they detected in their parents' faces. And they also had approached the meeting with fear and trembling.

After many hours of emotionally wrenching talking and listening, it began to be apparent that, in many ways, they were coming from the same place. They had all grown up under the shadow of their parents' trauma, carrying irrational anger, guilt and melancholia.

The "break" came after several days when one of the women, a child of death camp survivors, spoke directly to the son of a Nazi officer, telling him that much in her wanted to hate and reject him but, having heard his story, not too unlike her own, and having sensed his humanity in his demeanor, she wanted only to tell him that she loved him. Then it was that they shared a tearful hug, breaking the ice for the others, as well!

What they had experienced at the end of that week together was the power of forgiveness. It is this gift that Jesus includes in his Prayer as an epilogue to the many places in the Sermon that speak of forgiveness, reconciliation and forbearance in love:

> ... *If you are angry at another, you will be liable to judgment ... if you ["write them off"] you shall be liable to the [torment] ... if you bring a gift to the altar with a grudge against another, go and be reconciled first.*
> (Matthew 5:21f, author's paraphrase).

> ... *Love your enemies and pray for those who persecute you, so that you may be children of your Father in heaven for God makes his sun rise on the evil and the good.*
> (5:44-45)

> ... *If you forgive others, your heavenly Father will also forgive you.*　　　　　　　　　(6:14)

> ... *Do to others as you would have them do to you ... this is the law and the prophets.*　　　　(7:12)

It is plain that Jesus expects of his followers that they take the initiative in mending relationships, something that can be very difficult (seemingly impossible in some situations) without having the mind and spirit of Christ.

Here is a clear example of what we described before as the creative word of Jesus that does more than change our minds but begins heart-change, as well. All of our human instincts protest the implication that we must give peace and reconciliation first priority, even above justifiable retaliation or legitimate defense of personal pride. But the example of Jesus contradicts what would normally be expected. While he could be irritated at the abuse inflicted on others, as when he chastised the scribes and Pharisees for "devouring widow's houses"

(Matthew 23:14), his tolerance of abuse upon himself was legendary (see Matthew 27:27-44). One of his final words was forgiveness for his executioners (Luke 23:34).

One of the most extraordinary aspects of the Lord's Prayer forgiveness petition is the way forgiveness is used in context with indebtedness: "Forgive us our *debts* . . ." (Matthew 6:12), a phrase which is present in Luke's version as well as Matthew's.

For Discussion

One common version substitutes the word *trespasses* for *debts*. Does "trespasses" limit or expand the meaning of Jesus' petition for you? Do you feel that if you don't infringe (trespass) on someone else's property you have fulfilled the moral implication of Jesus' petition? Why or why not? Do you think there's any relationship between this petition and the mandate that you should "love your neighbor as yourself"?

The tone of the petition is significantly colored by its association with the twin petition seeking the forgiveness of God for ourselves. It is only those who gratefully receive the forgiveness of God for having failed God's hopes for *them* who can find it in their hearts to take the initiative in restoring peace to a broken relationship. The interpretive comment which follows the prayer in Matthew's account (Matthew 6:14-15), about God's forgiveness being contingent on our forgiveness of others, requires interpretation. To cast God as a score-keeping deity, as Job's friends did, is to ignore the picture of the parent-God which Jesus gave us. I understand Jesus to be telling us that our gracious God finds it very difficult to give forgiveness to a heart full of anger. And it is in that sense alone that one might say that God forgives in proportion to our acts of forgiveness. The important point that the teaching makes is that it is only a heart grateful for undeserved grace from God that can find it possible to take the initiative in forgiving and in seeking reconciliation.

Putting someone in debt to oneself is barely tolerated in the Bible. Should indebtedness be incurred against a person, there are clearly articulated rules defining how the indebtedness is to be repaid. Usury, the practice of loaning money for interest, is strictly forbidden between Hebrews (Leviticus 25:37). It is a practice easily abused by devious manipulation and hidden "terms." The law of the Sabbatical Year (Deuteronomy 15:1f) and the Year of Jubilee (Leviticus 25:10) were given by God to insure that indebtedness would be canceled at least every seven years and every 50 years so that debts would not be passed to succeeding generations.

For poor people, indebtedness often involved working as a slave in the creditor's household until the debt could be paid. Such "bonded servitude" was still common in the ancient world. Paul was uncomfortable with such an arrangement between Christians. He urged Philemon to pardon the runaway slave, Onesimus, and permit him to continue only as a useful and valued member of Philemon's family, as they were both brothers in the extended family, the church. "Keep him on not as a slave but as a brother," Paul urged (Philemon v. 16).

Research Activity

Read Jesus' parable of the Unforgiving Servant (Matthew 18:23-35). What do you think it says about Jesus' attitude toward the whole human debtor/creditor arrangement? Why does Jesus portray the creditor servant in such broad strokes? With whom does Jesus' sympathy lie? Have you ever had to endure unforgiveness from someone you valued? What was its effect on you? Was it resolved? How?

More importantly, Jesus makes the point that because the unforgiving servant was a recipient of the grace of the Master, he owed a debt of forgiveness to his impoverished fellow servant. Thus the one debt that God does not find irksome is introduced: the debt of neighborly love that we owe one another!

This parable, from Jesus' own lips, gives us an important clue about the forgiveness petition in the Lord's Prayer and the relevant Sermon passages. As forgiven sinners, we owe a debt of forgiveness that can never be repaid but which may repeatedly motivate us to forgive others.

Paul's great reconciliation passage in 2 Corinthians reasons in the same way:

> *If anyone is in Christ, there is a new creation: everything old has passed away; see, everything has become new! All this is from God, who reconciled us to himself through Christ, and has given us the ministry of reconciliation; that is, in Christ God was reconciling the world to himself, not counting their trespasses against them, and entrusted the message of reconciliation to us.*
>
> (2 Corinthians 5:17-19)

We choose forgiveness and reconciliation rather than incrimination and retaliation because God has so dealt with us!

This picture of *forgiven/forgiver* suggests some understandings that we may carry into our ministry of reconciliation. First, we refuse to be debilitated by carrying an unforgiving spirit. We refuse to expend energy and attention in nursing anger that could better be used in constructive behavior. Second, as we do not always accept God's forgiveness, hanging onto our guilt, we will understand when those to whom we offer "the olive branch" sometimes refuse it. As God does not stop being gracious, despite our reluctance to believe or receive it, so we will not stop being forgiving even when the other is slow to welcome it. We must "hang in" with this ministry of reconciliation. Lastly, our forgiveness is never contingent on the worthiness of the recipient. The stimulus for being forgiving is having been forgiven by God "while we were yet sinners" (Romans 5:8), not the worthiness or receptiveness of the recipient.

This means that Christians are called to interrupt the destructive cycles of retaliation and revenge that are behind so many conflicts and clashes. We are, in the imagery of the

Sermon on the Mount, to be the light, the salt, the leaven that prompts new and better ways of relating and actually changes things for the better.

Unison Prayer

O Holy One, by the power of your love and out of gratitude for your grace, prompt us to reflect your patience and forgiveness with one another. Because your love is endless and your grace inexhaustible, give us the largeness of heart we need to deal kindly with each other. Amen.

Questions For Discussion

1. How did you feel when you read the account of the Holocaust and Nazi offspring attempting dialogue? With whom did you identify the most? What might be a similar "insurmountable wall" for you?

2. Do you ever find your human instinct for self-justification resisting the implication that you must give peace and reconciliation first priority?

3. In what sense do we owe "an unpayable debt of forgiveness"?

Chapter 11

Relying On God's Leading

Matthew 5:27-47, 7:21-23, Luke 6:46-49

In the prologue to that powerful biblical saga, **Job,** God is pictured holding court, and the accuser, who has slipped in among the other heavenly beings who have come to pay homage, raises questions about the depth of Job's faith. He suggests that Job's is a "good times faith" that would collapse under testing. "Stretch out your hand now, and touch all that he has, and he will curse you to your face," taunts the accuser. God then rises to the challenge and permits the accuser to inflict Job with torment and loss, short of taking his life, "Very well, all that he has is in your power; only do not stretch your hand against *him*! (Job 1:11-12).

This remarkable book dares to question the common orthodox assumption that suffering is punishment for sin. Job's righteousness is never in question, only the depth of his faith under testing. His so-called friends call on him to reach into his past and find the sin that brought these calamities, and his wife, at one point, urges him to curse God and be done with it. Only Job sees that faith can persist even in the midst of inexplicable suffering, "Yea though he slay me, yet will I trust in him" (Job 13:15 KJV). Job does not abandon his hope that one day, without his flesh, he shall perceive God as on his side and not another (Job 19:26). It is the same faith that inspired a Jew hiding in a Cologne cellar during the Nazi purges, to scribble on the wall:

I believe in the sun,
  even when it is not shining;
I believe in love,
  even when not feeling it;

I believe in God,
  even when he is silent!

Jesus, like the writer of the 23rd Psalm, does not expect God to lead us *around* trouble or temptation but *through* it. A faith that cannot triumph through adversity is not the faith of Job, David or Jesus!

In keeping with our theme that proposes that the Lord's Prayer may be seen as an Epilogue to the Sermon on the Mount, we need to ask what the greatest temptations are from Jesus' perspective. And they may surprise you. For they have little to do with the keeping of rules and the practice of religion. Their focus is on relationships and on qualities like honesty, devotion, reverence, forgiveness and love.

There are three areas of relationship that are spotlighted in Jesus' Sermon: those with other persons, those with society and those with our Father in heaven. These provide the battleground upon which temptation assaults God's children.

The arena of person-to-person relationships provides the area of greatest vulnerability: to see another as an object for sexual gratification, when lust parades as love (Matthew 5:27); to take the marriage bond lightly (5:31); to hold on to anger, to nurse a grudge, to write people off, and to deceive through high sounding promises (5:27-42) — all behavior fracturing to qualitative relationships. All people are susceptible to such behavior: tax collectors and Pharisees, priests and common people, educated and uneducated, rich and poor.

To those who pretend to pureness of thought as well as action, Jesus suggests that the temptation to see others as sexual objects may come as a by-product of human nature. And to those who are serious about changing and have no pretense about immunity, Jesus says control it at the point of action. We may not be able always to redirect our thoughts but we can refuse to dwell on the thought or to act on the impulse. That I take to be the meaning of "If your right eye causes you to sin, tear it out and throw it away ... And if your right hand causes you to sin, cut it off and throw it away; it is better for you to lose one of your members than for your whole body to go into Gehenna [Greek: the garbage heap]'' (Matthew 5:29-30). Jesus spoke in hyperbole to grab attention and make an emphatic point, but there is nothing obscure about his advice.

For Discussion

Should you feel guilty about involuntary impulsive thoughts and fantasies? If not, what should you feel responsible for when you fail to meet your moral expectations for yourself? Is it your *behavior* for which you should be ultimately held accountable in light of Jesus' teaching in Matthew 5:29-30? Does this interpretation make you feel better or worse?

When we manage not to dwell on the temptation and not to act on the impulse and, furthermore, when we choose a better way of relating to that person, then it can truly be said that God has led us through temptation and delivered us from evil! That, says Jesus, should be our prayer and our resolve.

The second arena in which temptation is played out is the area of our social relationships. When we do things for show and when we dishonor certain groups in society categorically, we do not show that we are children of our Parent in heaven.

Jesus is aware that even potentially *good* practices — almsgiving, prayer and fasting — can be done not out of a desire for spiritual growth but in order to impress others. This was a particularly sensitive area for the pious elite. The pictures were familiar to any who might have spent a day in Jerusalem observing the antics of the ''holier than thou's'': trumpeters grandly heralding the almsgiver dropping his coins into the poorbox or the beggar's hat with grand gesture; the public prayer making sure he is the center of attention in the synagogue or the civic center; and the faster, walking around the public place, face smeared with ashes.

Jesus says, that for the true seeker, the audience is not the public but the Father. God ''who sees in secret will reward you'' (Matthew 6:4, 6, 18). The most reward for such public display might be the attention of the crowds. If, however, one is looking for the blessing of *God*, then the offering, the prayer, the fasting must be a matter of our heart to God's heart, personal and, insofar as possible, private. For ''the true worshipper worships the Father in spirit and in truth'' (John 4:23). To ''make points'' in terms of recognition, prestige or reputation by religious exhibitionism is one of the most insidious of temptations! To Jesus religious pretense was one of the most serious sins.

Research Activity

Read Matthew 5:46-47. To which two groups, disdained by the pious Jew, does Jesus specifically refer? How would you feel to be compared unfavorably with two groups of people you hold in dishonor? Of what groups might Jesus be speaking suitably in your case? What kind of response might Jesus be wanting from you?

It appears that Jesus could not get through this Sermon without touching the pretenders at one of their most sensitive points: their prejudices. In doing so, Jesus is suggesting that this is also an arena of great temptation: categorically rejecting certain groups or classes of people as unworthy of either our respect or God's care.

The third arena in which we are most vulnerable to temptation is that of our relationship to God. It should be clear by now that a large part of this Sermon has to do with our understanding of and approach to the Parent in heaven. Jesus' picture is of a God who is impartial with God's gifts, ''He makes his sun to shine and his rain to fall on the righteous and the unrighteous'' (Matthew 5:45). God, for Jesus, is a Parent who is eager to give God's children good things, is ready to hear our prayers and reward our sincere acts of worship, and who is ready to forgive us and guide us. ''Your Father in heaven will give good things to those who ask him'' (7:11). If we strive first for the Realm of God and God's righteousness, all the things necessary for a good life will be given to us as well (6:33).

In light of that understanding of God, it is doubly incomprehensible how religion can become a sham, a pretense, a display and a show!

Research Activity

See how Jesus parodies such behavior in Matthew 7:21-23. How is this temptation, as Jesus describes it, one that comes mainly to church people like ourselves? In what way are our good deeds tainted by desire for God's approval and rewards?

To become self-conscious and ambitious in one's religious practices, to justify one's prejudices and one's old behavior on religious rationalizations, to tabulate one's good deeds in anticipation of some sort of pay-off, and to believe that God's favor can be coerced by pretensions of goodness are rarely temptations that come to the impious! Jesus' harshest words were reserved for those who were self-righteous and counted themselves better than others.

> *On the outside you look righteous to others, but on the inside you are full of hypocrisy and lawlessness.*
> (Matthew 23:28)

These sins of relationship in the areas of person to person, person to society and person to God can be faced and overcome by faith in God who can "lead us not into temptation but deliver us from evil." In such confidence, the Apostle Paul proclaimed, "I can do all things through him that *strengtheneth* me" (Philippians 4:13).

If we look for a smooth path, with all the obstructions removed, we are in for disappointment, for God leads us *through* temptation, as God did with Job and as God did with Jesus and Paul.

Reinhold Niebuhr, in a prayer that has become important in the Alcoholics Anonymous program, captures some of the meaning of the "lead us" petition:

> *Grant me, O Lord, the serenity to accept those things I cannot change; the courage to change those things that can be changed; and the wisdom to distinguish one from the other.*

That it is a prayer addressed to *the Lord* is of equal importance to the petitions themselves. For it is the Lord who gives courage, who picks up where *our* ability to change things leaves off, and who grants wisdom that accepts our human limitations even as it trusts in the unlimited power and unfailing love of our Parent in heaven!

The saga of Job is not the only place in scripture where God permits God's own to be led into temptation. Jesus was led "by the Spirit into the wilderness to be tempted by the devil" (Matthew 4:1) before he was ready to take up his messianic ministry. The writer of Hebrews finds great encouragement for Christians in this fact, saying:

> *... he had become like his brothers and sisters in every respect, so that he might be a merciful and faithful high priest in the service of God, to make a sacrifice of atonement for the sins of the people. **Because he himself was tempted by what he suffered, he is able to help those who are being tested** .... For we do not have a high priest who is unable to sympathize with our weaknesses, but we have one who in **every respect has been tempted as we are,** yet without [succumbing]. Let us therefore approach the throne of grace with boldness, so that we may receive help in time of need.*
>
> (Hebrews 2:17-18, 4:14-15)

That's what we do in the "lead us" petition of the Lord's Prayer: approach the throne of grace with confidence, so that we may receive help to go through temptation, even as the Lord went through it, and, like him, be stronger because of it!

Questions For Discussion

1. Is the idea that the Lord's Prayer petitions God to lead us *through* rather than around temptation a new one for you? What difference does it make for you?

2. How is "a faith that cannot triumph through adversity" not the faith of Job or Jesus?

3. Have you found the Niebuhr (A.A.) prayer personally useful? In what way?

Chapter 12

An "Amen" People

Matthew 6:9-13, 7:24-27, Luke 6:47-49

When we say "Amen" to the Lord's Prayer, we are petitioning God to "make it so" or "let it be." If, then, the Lord's Prayer is, as we've suggested in this writing, a "cameo" of the Sermon on the Mount, we are subscribing to the radical, culture-challenging ethics of Jesus!

We have spoken to its major themes: the central understanding of God as Parent, the gracious/persuasive as opposed to the vengeful/coercive One, whose name is worthy of honor. That is, God's name is not to be used for pretense, for show, or for manipulative purposes. We have seen how God's Realm celebrates humility, peaceableness, service, honesty, and the honoring of commitment in relationships. We have heard Jesus' call for a life of simplicity and daily trust in God — "our daily bread" — urging us to share the earth's fruits with others. We have perceived the need for a forgiving nature, so that we take the initiative in reconciliation, and are open about our own shortcomings. We have heard the call to take God with us *through* the places of trial and temptation, and to endure suffering in anticipation of deliverance. And we have reaffirmed God's power to overcome human resistance and achieve the building of God's Realm.

The plain inference of the placement of the Lord's Prayer at the heart of this compendium of Jesus' teachings, the Sermon on the Mount, is that those who commit themselves to the Teacher and his teachings will "pray in this manner" (Matthew 6:9)! When we pray in the manner of the Lord's Prayer we are "signing on" to those values, those principles and that way of life!

I will never forget the first time I heard the exclamation, "Amen!" when I was filling the pulpit in an African-American church. It caught me off guard. It indicated that someone was actually hearing what I was saying and joining me in making the point to the others! Someone was saying "so be it" to a point I was making, and I almost had to stop and look again at what I had said! I discovered that in at least one tradition the teachings were being considered for their practical value in the life of a Christian. I had become so used to moving air waves above poker faces and sleepy heads that it no longer occurred to me that someone might be seriously listening for a word from the Lord for their lives!

"Amen" or "so be it" is more than a call to God to take over and, unilaterally, do magic work to bring your petitions to pass. "Amen" is a recognition that when our will is at last in harmony with God's will, we will work in partnership with God to bring about the things for which we have fervently prayed. It represents an active not a passive faith stance. It would not be unfair to say that, with respect to where it sits in the Sermon on the Mount, the Lord's Prayer means, "Enlist me in making it so!"

Have you noticed that in Matthew 6:9-13 there is no *amen* after the Lord's Prayer? Jesus implies that the *amen* has to come from us, as a response to the Lord's Prayer.

Be careful when you say "Amen" to the Lord's Prayer, especially if you are unwilling to be part of the solution for which you have just prayed.

If all of us who routinely recite the Lord's Prayer were to see it as a sign of commitment to the radical, culture-challenging ethics of the Sermon on the Mount, many of us would, I dare say, revert to, "Now I lay me down to sleep . . . ."

There is a better alternative. We may study again the teachings of Jesus and hear, as if for the first time, the call for us to be peacemakers, to have a mellowing effect on the world, to stand for honesty, truthfulness, integrity and loyalty in human relationships, to practice our faith and worship God not in order to impress others but "in spirit and in truth," and to give the unexpected response to enemies, exploiters and those in authority.

We can do this with the understanding that Jesus is committed to us as we give our minds and hearts to him and his teachings.

Research Activity

See what Jesus says to those who take seriously his call to live as children of God in John 15:16-18 and 16:7-8. Does Jesus promise that his values will cease to seem "topsy-turvy" to the world? What *does* he promise to those who are committed to his understanding of sin, righteousness and justice?

Jesus will not leave comfortless those who are seeking to show his mind and his spirit in their living.

When a grass roots theology emerged from the poor and oppressed of Latin America in the '70s, there was skepticism and snobbery on the part of those who had been interpreting theology in doctrinal and theoretical ways. They called it naive and one-dimensional, lacking in theological depth. What we are beginning to see now is that this theology was calling us back to something essential about the teaching of Jesus that we were missing: that his is a practical theology.

If there is any truth to one church historian's conclusion that the earliest followers centered on the social experiment called for by Jesus' fresh, culture-challenging teachings, then it is possible that this grass roots theology is closer to the truth than conventional institutional theology. Perhaps Jesus would be more at home in the cells and house churches of the poor than in the lecture halls of North American seminaries. We know he is at home in the hearts of those committed to be his instruments in the world.

In his book *Compassion*, Henri Nouwen says:

> *There is little doubt that the disciples of Jesus understood their call as a call to make God's compassion present in this world by moving with Jesus into positions of servant-hood.* (p. 28)

Only in this context does the presence of the Lord's Prayer in the Sermon on the Mount make sense. Those who are set free to practice the ethics of the Sermon on the Mount — forgiveness, love (even for those hardest to love), humility, honesty and generosity — are those who will pray in the manner of the Lord's Prayer, and put their body where their prayer is. They are free to live compassionately in servanthood, their hand in his hand.

Questions For Discussion

1. Do you agree that in the case of the "Amen" on the Lord's Prayer you are subscribing to the radical, culture-challenging ethics of the Sermon on the Mount and the Realm of God?

2. When is it appropriate for you to say "Amen"?

3. What kind of commitment does Jesus make to you when you try to be faithful to his instructions?

4. Has seeing the parallel between Latin American "liberation theology" and Jesus' strong social consciousness given you reason to take a second look at it? What have those theologians taught us?

---

1. McNeill, Morrison, Nouwen, *Compassion* (New York: Doubleday and Co., 1982), p. 78.